ideals®
CHRISTMAS

More Than 50 Years of Celebrating Life's Most Treasured Moments

Vol. 56, No. 6

"Christians, awake! Salute the happy morn
Whereon the Saviour of the world was born."—John Byrom

Featured Photograph 6	A Slice of Life 26	Our Heritage 64
Country Chronicle 9	Devotions from the Heart 32	Collector's Corner 70
From My Garden Journal 12	The Christmas Story 36	Legendary Americans 74
Remember When 16	Through My Window 48	Traveler's Diary 76
For the Children 18	Handmade Heirloom 54	Bits and Pieces 82
Readers' Reflections 24	Ideals' Family Recipes 60	Readers' Forum 86

IDEALS—Vol. 56, No. 6 November MCMXCIX IDEALS (ISSN 0019-137X) is published six times a year: January, March, May, July, September, and November by
IDEALS PUBLICATIONS INCORPORATED,
535 Metroplex Drive, Suite 250, Nashville, TN 37211.
Periodical postage paid at Nashville, Tennessee, and additional mailing offices.
Copyright © MCMXCIX by IDEALS PUBLICATIONS INCORPORATED.
POSTMASTER: Send address changes to Ideals, PO Box 305300,
Nashville, TN 37230. All rights reserved.

Title IDEALS registered U.S. Patent Office.
SINGLE ISSUE—U.S. $5.95 USD; Higher in Canada
ONE-YEAR SUBSCRIPTION—U.S. $19.95 USD; Canada $36.00 CDN (incl. GST and shipping); Foreign $25.95 USD
TWO-YEAR SUBSCRIPTION—U.S. $35.95 USD; Canada $66.50 CDN (incl. GST and shipping); Foreign $47.95 USD

Subscribers may call customer service at 1-800-558-4343 to make address changes.
Unsolicited manuscripts will not be returned without a self-addressed, stamped envelope.

ISBN 0-8249-1158-X   GST 131903775

Cover Photo
CHRISTMAS AT STONE CHAPEL
Artist, Linda Nelson Stocks

Inside Front Cover
Nostalgic greeting card
Image from David
Spindel/Superstock

Inside Back Cover
Musical angel
Image from Superstock

WHEN WINTER COMES

John C. Bonser

When winter visits us at last
with many an icy, chilling blast
and scatters mounds of fallen leaves
until they hide in shrubs and eaves,
we mourn the gentle seasons past.

When snow comes down for many days
and hills are cloaked in silver haze,
when all the ground is frozen hard
and slippery slopes put us on guard,
we rail at winter's devious ways.

And yet, when winter brings as well
a log fire's own delightful smell
and rosy cheeks on each small face
as children play outside our place,
the snowballs fly and targets yell.

We find that winter's not so bad
but offers much to make us glad:
fond memories of holidays—
with loved ones shared in many ways—
that once in wintertime we had.

LEFT: A home in Geneva, Illinois, welcomes winter guests. Photo by Jessie Walker. ABOVE: A child is bundled up for a dog sled ride across the Alaska snow. Photo by Jane Gnass/Gnass Photo Images.

GLASS
DISPLAY

Inez Franck

The sugared world is white and cold
As Nature shows her glass display;
The cedar boughs, icicle-hung,
Resemble chandeliers today.

The lake is like a mirror set
Upon the frozen countryside;
The waterfalls, so placid still,
Are pitchers iced for summer's pride.

The snowflakes make a crystal bowl
Where sparrows wing to take a bath;
The hollow log becomes a vase
For winter berries on the path.

I cannot miss each fragile piece
That traps and mirrors rays of light;
Come look with me before the sun
Can break this very sheer delight.

LEFT: A thrifty squirrel nibbles a berry in the Boston Public Garden. Photo by Dianne Dietrich Leis. OVERLEAF: A snow-covered footbridge reflects in a winter pond in Seattle's Kubota Gardens. Photo by Mary Liz Austin.

Country
CHRONICLE
Lansing Christman

DECEMBER SUNSETS

I have yet to see two sunsets precisely alike, and each enchanting display fills me with wonder and awe. The close of each day inspires me as I gaze at the western horizon painted in hues of red and pink and gold. I watch as the sun slips down behind the hills and unfurls a spectacular banner across the sky.

Sunsets in any season are fascinating. The colors seem to vary with the seasons—clear and sharp in fall and winter, less spectacular in spring and summer. Cold-weather sunsets enhance the artistry of the display, and I am especially awed by the haunting beauty of December sunsets.

The change begins in October, when the harvest moon shines down on a field of corn shocks and leaves wigwam-like shadows under the mellow glow. The air is keen and clear, sharp with frosted jewels on leaf and stem. The colors glow vivid and pure and imbue me with profound inspiration.

I watched a recent sunset when a mass of broken clouds, some dark, some fleecy and fluffy and light, hovered over the long expanse of the horizon. The drowsy clouds swallowed the sun as it pushed its remaining visible light up into the sky like the wick of a lamp pushing its flame up into the shining globe.

December sunsets. They are a time for dreams, yearning dreams that tug at the heart. These dreams come by watching the painted sky as it hovers silently over the Carolina hills.

The author of three published books, Lansing Christman has been contributing to Ideals *for almost thirty years. Mr. Christman has also been published in several American, foreign, and braille anthologies. He lives in rural South Carolina.*

American artist Walter Launt Palmer (1854–1932) captures the glow of a December sunset in TWILIGHT. *Image from Christie's Images/Superstock.*

Portrait of Winter

Brian F. King

Now, blissfully, the woodlands dream
Where winter crowns each sleeping hill;
Where silent shadows blend and twine
In drowsy valleys, white and still.

Now, tinkling brooklets softly sing
Sweet slumber songs to snows that lie
Where seedlings dream of spring to come
Beneath a bleak December sky.

Contentment dwells where nature's hand
Has sketched a winter wonderland.

Snowfall

Louise Pugh Corder

The snow fell softly in the night,
Adorned the trees in robes of white,
Bowed graceful branches to the ground,
And frosted earth without a sound,
Etched fragile stars on windowpane,
Spread fluffy carpet on the lane.

Of barren field there is no trace;
The whole farm wears a fresh new face.
The orchard, mill, and fence all look
Like pictures in a storybook.
The Lord has wrapped the earth in snow
And set my winter heart aglow.

*Mabry Mill anchors this majestic winter scene on Virginia's
Blue Ridge Parkway. Photo by Norman Poole.*

Deana Deck

CHRISTMAS ROSE

I consider myself blessed when I find a friend who shares my love of gardening, someone who actually enjoys talking about compost and who will offer extra plants from her own garden to replace unlucky ones in mine. So I was doubly sad when a green-thumb friend of mine recently moved out of town. Yet before her house was sold, she divided and shared with me many of the perennials that she had spent the last six years cultivating in her small yard. Among the plants was one I had often admired but never grown: an old, beloved garden plant called the Christmas rose.

Through the years, the popularity of the Christmas rose (*Helleborus niger*) has had much to do with its interesting history. Also called *hellebore* or winter rose, the plant was valued by the ancient Greeks for medicinal use. One myth led to it being considered a treatment for insanity; when Proteus, god of the

sea, engaged the physician Melampus to treat his mad daughters, the physician treated the girls with hellebore. John Gerard, in his herbal manual written in 1597, declared that hellebore was a good treatment for "mad and furious men." The hellebore was considered so magical it became popular as a means of cleansing homes of any evil spirits.

A more endearing legend explains how the hellebore acquired its common name. On the night that Christ was born, word of the Messiah's birth spread throughout the countryside. A small shepherd girl named Madelon heard of the holy birth and walked to Bethlehem to see the Christ Child. Because she had no gift for the Babe, she remained outside the manger, crying softly in shame. When God saw the little girl, He took pity on her. Though she was poor and humble, He recognized that her heart was filled with love, so He sent the angel Gabriel to help her. Gabriel touched the hard barren soil around Madelon, and she was immediately surrounded by dozens of beautiful white flowers. Relieved and happy, the child picked a large bouquet, softly approached the Christ Child, and laid the blossoms beside him in the manger. Ever since that night, the plant has been known as the Christmas rose.

Knowing this legend of the Christmas rose, I was honored to give my friend's plant a home in my own garden. We transplanted her Christmas rose in May, not the best time for any perennial, especially one that dislikes being moved. My friend's plants, however, are always healthy and robust, so I was not entirely surprised when the hellebore thrived and even bloomed in my yard. I was unprepared, however, for the great

CHRISTMAS ROSE

mass of flowers that appeared and lingered. From early fall until late spring, the plant continued to bloom and I continued to enjoy it.

I soon learned that some gardeners report that under perfect conditions, a Christmas rose will produce blooms nearly year round. These conditions aren't hard to achieve: sandy, neutral soil rich in humus, winter sun, summer shade, and ample water throughout the year.

These conditions mimic the plant's native conditions in the Balkans and Italy's Dolomite and Apennine Mountains. The Christmas rose has climate preferences similar to the tulip and the lilac; it enjoys a bit of winter chill. My Zone 6 climate enjoys fairly mild winters, but each January we tend to get a few weeks of real winter. Temperatures plunge to single digits, outdoor plants freeze, and the soil reaches temperatures cool enough to keep most cool-season perennials, such as the Christmas rose, happy and thriving. Further south, the plant does best in higher altitudes. In colder parts of the country, it actually blooms in the snow.

In spite of its name, the Christmas rose will usually produce a mass of creamy white flowers from November through April.

The Christmas rose is an evergreen plant about twelve to eighteen inches tall, with glossy leaves deeply divided into seven to nine leaflets. The flowers are creamy white with bright yellow stamens and can be as wide as two inches across. As the blossoms age, they turn faintly pink or purplish. Even the flower stalks of this plant are attractive: fleshy and red-spotted, carrying up to three pure white, cup-shaped flowers per stem. In spite of its name, the Christmas rose will usually bloom continuously from November through April. One variety, Praecox, is reputed to bloom as early as October and is hardy to Zone 5.

Later-blooming varieties of the Christmas rose are called Lenten roses (*H. Orientalis*). These are just as attractive but bear several blooms on a single stalk and have slightly smaller blossoms. The Lenten rose is native to Turkey and Greece and is available in a wide range of colors, from creamy white to pink and magenta. It produces blooms in March and April, but maintains a bold, evergreen presence in the garden all year. The blossoms first appear with nodding, downward-facing blooms, but they gradually become horizontal or upright. Lenten roses are good companion plants to add to your bed of Christmas roses since the bloom periods of the two plants will often overlap.

The Christmas rose is generally easy to care for and enjoys a deep feeding of composted manure in spring. The plant can be divided in fall, but it must be handled very carefully due to its brittle root system. It does best when a large ball of soil is moved with the roots. Although some references claim it does not thrive for two or three years after being divided, this is not the case if diligent care is exercised when digging and moving the plant.

This winter I am looking forward to enjoying the blooms from my own transplanted Christmas rose. My plant may not have been given to me by an angel of God, as was the case with Madelon; but it was a gift from an angelic friend who realized how a dozen white blossoms can warm a winter heart.

Deana Deck tends to her flowers, plants, and vegetables at her home in Nashville, Tennessee, where her popular garden column is a regular feature in The Tennessean.

Childhood Christmas

June R. Collins

The tree with its candles cheerful and bright
Has etched itself deeply in memory's sight.
The toys were not many, the fare was not grand,
But I was the luckiest child in the land.

The snow sparkled sharply outside the door,
And the house a bright mantle of icicles wore.
But the inside was warm with the love that was there
With a spirit of giving and wanting to share.

The popcorn was strung and the cranberries too;
The shabby old ornaments even looked new.
The story of Christmas was read to us all,
And the carols we sang I still can recall.

Then snuggled in bed on a cold Christmas night
And up with the first of the dawn's faintest light.
Yes, there stood the tree, the most beautiful ever;
It was and it is and it will be forever.

It is good to be children sometimes and never better than at Christmas.

—*Charles Dickens*

A simple tree holds gifts for a lucky child on Christmas morn. Photo by Jessie Walker.

Remember When

THE PERILS AND PLEASURES OF WINTER

Marjorie Holmes

An old fashioned, family kind of winter brings back all the Christmases past that I knew as a little girl. It brings back the winter sports that were the glorious preview: the ice skating, the snow battles, the hopping of bobs. An entire new era of delight was ushered in with the first snowfall; and with the freezing of the lake, it became an intense reality.

The lake, that vast rolling body of water in which we had frolicked all summer, became forbidden territory soon after Labor Day. Though it continued to rush shoreward with foaming force, we knew that the days of its might were numbered. Winter was watching from behind the gold, then gradually naked, trees. Soon the water would lie subdued, the first sheets of ice inching out from the shore. Every day some daring boy would test its surface, racing back at the sounds of cracking. But the cold and certain encroachment was taking place; until one day, after severe nights and several false reports, the word would race through town: "The lake's frozen over!" And though parents remained doubtful and issued edicts and warnings, the first few figures began taking tentative swings across its glassy expanse.

"Fools," our dad would declare. "You kids aren't setting foot on that ice until we're sure it's safe."

"But is is!" we'd claim. "Old Doc Vanderhoof's been going out every day."

Old Vanderhoof, a retired "horse doctor," was also our local Hans Brinker. Dutch-born, a superb skater, whenever you saw that tubby figure, arms folded, white whiskers blowing, doing his loops and turns, the parents were assured. The ice was safe.

Our skates had been ready for days, dug out from cellar, barn or attic, sharpened, polished, their worn straps tested, tried on repeatedly. "Now take those things off," Mother scolded, as we clumped or wob-

bled about. "You'll cut the rug and you'll scar the floor." Each year we inherited bigger ones from older brothers and sisters, and passed ours down. Or you traded with the neighbors. Sometimes the purchase of a new pair was not to be avoided; and oh the thrill of those tough, strong, leathery-smelling straps, the brilliance of the blades.

We lived only two blocks from the lake. On Saturdays, and most days after school, we hastened down to The Point, a favorite gathering place. Here an old green boathouse afforded shelter from the stinging blasts. It was always intensely cold; and though we were lumpy with long underwear and bundled to the eyebrows in layers of sweaters, jackets, leggings, mufflers, mittens, we huddled in its protection, or drew gratefully toward the great crackling fire that older boys often built among the rocks.

Armed with stubby brooms, the boys would have swept the snow aside for a hockey court. And what blithe young [men] they seemed as they smacked the little puck with their store-bought or homemade hockey sticks, laughing, yelling, fighting with a fierce and joyous abandon.

Boys also fought pitched battles behind their snow forts, and here the girls were allowed, if only in the capacity of providing ammunition. Our job was to make the snowballs, and we gloated over our growing stock, much as our mothers proudly counted their canning. A good snowball maker was much in demand. I always envied Gert Beatty who was first to be chosen when she trudged out. She fashioned round, firm snowballs with the same methodical skill that she turned out loaves of bread for her mother. Hers put my leaky, lopsided snowballs to shame. An even higher honor was accorded Kac Ford, a girl who knew more about football than most boys and had such a terrific pitching arm she was not only allowed on the team, she sometimes led the charge.

Two young friends prepare to brave a ride down Miller's hill in this vintage photo from Superstock.

Yet for sheer exhilarating delight, nothing could equal hitching bobsled rides. With the onset of winter, cars were hoisted onto blocks to protect the tires and stored away. There were simply no facilities for sweeping the snow-muffled streets. Townspeople walked (or waded) to their destination; country people traveled by bob. Saturday was the big trading day in town and, consequently, the best day for hopping bobs. Farmers approaching Storm Lake by almost any road were met by a swarm of kids, most of them pulling sleds. If you didn't have a sled, you hopped on the long wooden runner and hung onto the wagon box. With a sled you looped its rope over a bolt at the back or through a brace at its side.

Parents were always issuing futile edicts against the hopping of bobs. Yet they too remembered the thrill of lying belly-flat upon a sled that went whistling and bouncing across the crusty and glittering ground—here bumpy, here glass smooth, here grayly tramped, here purest shining white, while up front there was the steady plocking rhythm of the horses' hooves, the jingle of harness, the creak and rattle of the wagon box, while sometimes wisps of straw flew back like pinfeathers from angel wings.

Clutching the wooden rudders of our sleds, we steered, avoiding the deeper ruts and, rounding a corner, trying not to swing too far to the side. You could lose your grip, skid off, hit a curb, a lamppost, or be hurled into the path of an oncoming team. Thus the perils of a childhood winter, tempering our pleasure, yet enhancing it.

FOR THE CHILDREN

CHRISTMAS SLED

Author Unknown

Oh for the winters that used to be,
The winters that only a boy may see!
Rich with the snowflakes' rush and swirl,
Keen as a diamond, pure as a pearl,
Brimming with healthful, rollicking fun,
Sweet with their rest when the play was done.
With kindly revels each day decreed,
And a CHRISTMAS SLED for the royal steed.

Down from the crest with a shrill HURRAY—
Clear the track there! OUT OF THE WAY!
Scarcely touching the path beneath;
Scarcely admitting of breath to breathe.
Dashing along with leap and swerve,
Over the crossing, round the curve,
Talk of your flying machines! Instead,
Give me the SWOOP of that Christmas sled.

A thrilling sled ride becomes a happy winter memory in DOWNHILL
DELIGHT *by American artist Donald Zolan. Copyright © Zolan Fine Arts,
Ltd., Hershey, Pennsylvania.*

FIRST CHRISTMAS

Betty W. Stoffel

Dear son, you're far too small to know
What sets the Christmas heart aglow.
You'll only look with grave surprise
As colors dance before your eyes.
The manger scene, the lighted star,
The greeting cards from near and far,
The splendor of a lovely tree,
The carols of eternity,
These shall be meaningless this year
To little eye and little ear.

First Christmas! O my tiny son,
For me it is a special one;
For I, who hold you close, have trod
Those sacred steps that lead to God.
And so, for both of us, I know
What sets the Christmas heart aglow;
So I shall see and I shall hear
For both of us this Christmas, dear.
I feel so close to Him through you,
For once God's Son was little too.

A CHRISTMAS LULLABY

Lelia Watson

Sleep, little baby of mine,
Night and the darkness are near.
Nestled so close in my arms,
Baby has nothing to fear.
The lambs are asleep in the fold,
On the hillside the cattle at rest,
And you in my arms I hold.
Sleep, little bird, in your nest.

Once in Bethlehem-town,
A Baby as lovely, my sweet,
Slept in His mother's arms
And angels sang Him to sleep.
That was long, long ago, little lamb,
But Mary her vigil still keeps;
And the Baby who slept in her arms
Now watches my babe while he sleeps.

Sleep, baby, sleep! The mother sings:
Heaven's angels kneel and fold their wings.
Sleep, baby, sleep!

—*John Addington Symonds*

A rocking horse awaits a child's first Christmas morning. Photo by Greg Strelecki/International Stock.

THE CHRISTMAS TREE

Virginia Borman Grimmer

A forgotten Christmas tree
Sat lonely in the wood;
It wasn't chosen to adorn
Some parlor as it could.
It wanted to be beautiful,
Bedecked with baubles bright,
And lit at night with fancy globes
To be a splendid sight.
The birds and forest creatures
Must have known its woe,
For soon there came upon it
Two rabbits and a doe.
They bedded down on needles
Beneath the lonesome pine,
And birds flew on the branches
As if by great design.
And an iridescent bluebird
Made a sudden stop
On the very tallest branches;
It made a brilliant top.
Soft snowflakes started falling,
And soon, all flocked in white,
The little tree was lovely,
And quite an awesome sight.
For there was not a parlor
Anywhere in the land
That had a little Christmas tree
More stately or more grand.

*Snow perfectly drapes a hill of trees in this
photo by W. Otto/H. Armstrong Roberts.*

Readers' Reflections

Celebrate
Betty Wallace Scott
Akron, Ohio

Love tied up with a big red bow,
Joy in singing the songs we know,
Peace in the quiet fall of snow—
It's Christmas!

Light from the Star of Bethlehem,
Goodwill blessing every man,
Hope encircling the world again—
It's Christmas!

Mistletoe Kisses
Patti Merrill
Camp Verde, Arizona

Angel wings, candy canes,
mistletoe kisses;
Green and red ribbons
and sweet little misses;
Boys with their eyes shining bright
and girls giggling gaily;
Sometimes I almost
wish Christmas came daily!

Christmas Story
Gloria Trapold Bradford
Portland, Oregon

Christmas time with all its glory,
Tells us of that age-old story.
Bethlehem, a stable manger,
Mary, Joseph, a tiny stranger.
Shepherds, wise men, angels singing,

To all the world their message bringing.
Up in the sky that silent night
Shone a star so big and bright.
It told us all that it was done;
God had given us His son.

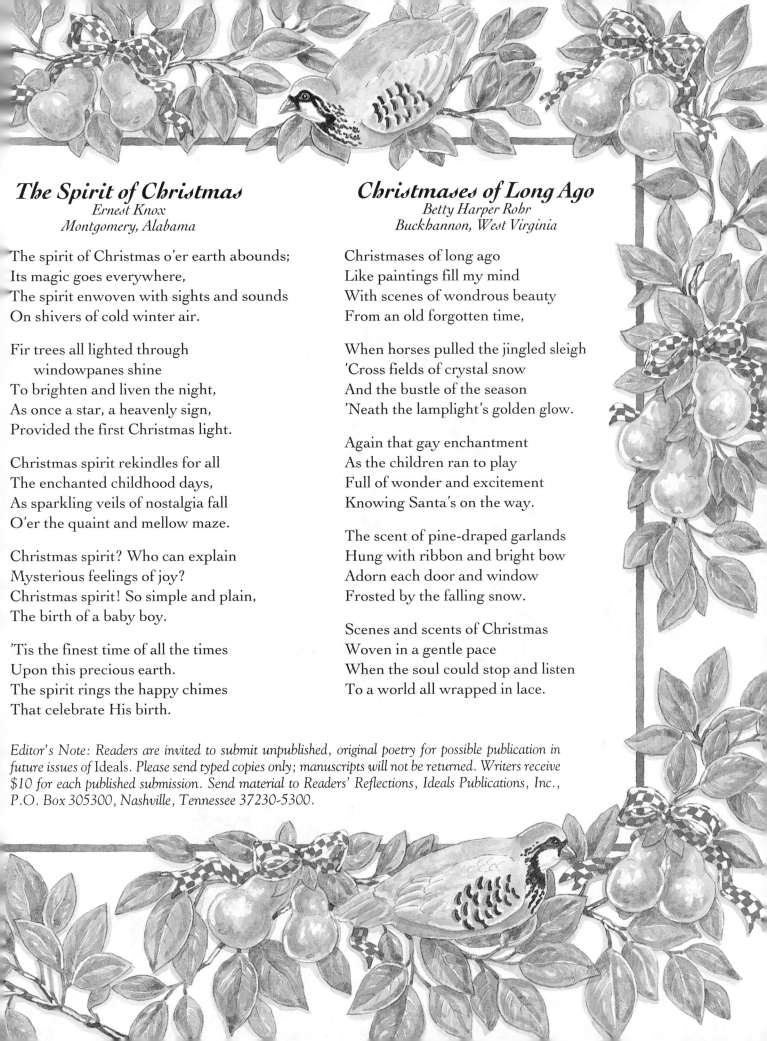

The Spirit of Christmas
Ernest Knox
Montgomery, Alabama

The spirit of Christmas o'er earth abounds;
Its magic goes everywhere,
The spirit enwoven with sights and sounds
On shivers of cold winter air.

Fir trees all lighted through
    windowpanes shine
To brighten and liven the night,
As once a star, a heavenly sign,
Provided the first Christmas light.

Christmas spirit rekindles for all
The enchanted childhood days,
As sparkling veils of nostalgia fall
O'er the quaint and mellow maze.

Christmas spirit? Who can explain
Mysterious feelings of joy?
Christmas spirit! So simple and plain,
The birth of a baby boy.

'Tis the finest time of all the times
Upon this precious earth.
The spirit rings the happy chimes
That celebrate His birth.

Christmases of Long Ago
Betty Harper Rohr
Buckhannon, West Virginia

Christmases of long ago
Like paintings fill my mind
With scenes of wondrous beauty
From an old forgotten time,

When horses pulled the jingled sleigh
'Cross fields of crystal snow
And the bustle of the season
'Neath the lamplight's golden glow.

Again that gay enchantment
As the children ran to play
Full of wonder and excitement
Knowing Santa's on the way.

The scent of pine-draped garlands
Hung with ribbon and bright bow
Adorn each door and window
Frosted by the falling snow.

Scenes and scents of Christmas
Woven in a gentle pace
When the soul could stop and listen
To a world all wrapped in lace.

Editor's Note: Readers are invited to submit unpublished, original poetry for possible publication in future issues of Ideals. *Please send typed copies only; manuscripts will not be returned. Writers receive $10 for each published submission. Send material to Readers' Reflections, Ideals Publications, Inc., P.O. Box 305300, Nashville, Tennessee 37230-5300.*

A
SLICE OF LIFE

Edgar A. Guest

SNOOPING 'ROUND

Last night I caught him on his knees and looking underneath the bed,
    And oh, the guilty look he wore, and oh, the stammered words he said,
When I, pretending to be cross, said: "Hey, young fellow, what's your game?"
    As if, back in the long ago, I hadn't also played the same;

As if, upon my hands and knees, I hadn't many a time been found
　　When, thinking of the Christmas Day, I'd gone upstairs to snoop around.

But there he stood and hung his head; the rascal knew it wasn't fair.
　　"I jes' was wonderin'," he said, "jes' what it was that's under there.
It's somepin' all wrapped up an' I thought mebbe it might be a sled,
　　Becoz I saw a piece of wood 'at's stickin' out all painted red."
"If Mother knew, " I said to him, "you'd get a licking, I'll be bound,
　　But just clear out of here at once, and don't you ever snoop around."

And as he scampered down the stairs, I stood and chuckled to myself,
　　As I remembered how I'd oft explored the top-most closet shelf.
It all came back again to me—with what a shrewd and cunning way
　　I too had often sought to solve the mysteries of Christmas Day.
How many times my daddy too had come upstairs without a sound.
　　And caught me just as I'd begun my clever scheme to snoop around.

And oh, I envied him his plight; I envied him the joy he feels
　　Who knows that every drawer that's locked some treasure dear
　　　　to him conceals;
I envied him his Christmas fun and wished that it again were mine
　　To seek to solve the mysteries, by paper wrapped and bound by twine.
Some day he'll come to understand that all the time I stood and frowned,
　　I saw a boy of years ago who also used to snoop around.

Edgar A. Guest began his illustrious career in 1895 at the age of fourteen when his work first appeared in the Detroit Free Press. *His column was syndicated in over three hundred newspapers, and he became known as "The Poet of the People."*

PAT THOMPSON

Annie and Willie's Prayer

Sophie P. Snow

'Twas the eve before Christmas; goodnight had
    been said,
And Annie and Willie had crept into bed.
There were tears on their pillows and tears in
    their eyes,
And each little bosom was heaving with sighs;
For tonight their stern father's command had
    been given
That they should retire precisely at seven
Instead of at eight; for they troubled him more
With questions unheard of ever before.
He told them he thought this delusion a sin—
No such thing as Santa Claus ever had been.
And he hoped, after this, he would never
    more hear
How he scrambled down chimneys with
    presents each year.

And this was the reason that two little heads
    So restlessly tossed on their soft,
    downy beds.
    Eight, nine, and the clock in the steeple
    tolled ten;
Not a word had been spoken by either till then.
When Willie's sad face from the blanket did peep
And whispered, "Dear Annie, is you fast asleep?"
"Why no, brother Willie," a sweet voice replied,
"I've tried in vain, but I can't shut my eyes.
For somehow it makes me so sorry because
Dear Papa said there is no Santa Claus;
Now we know that there is, and it can't be denied,
For he came every year before Mamma died.
But then I am thinking that she used to pray,
And God would hear everything Mamma
    would say.
And perhaps she asked Him to send Santa
    Claus here
With the sacks full of presents he brought
    every year."

"Well, why tan't we pray dest as Mamma did then

And ask Him to send him presents aden?"
"I've been thinking so too." And without
    a word more,
Four little bare feet bounded out on the floor.
Four little knees the soft carpet pressed,
And two tiny hands were clasped close
    to each breast.
"Now, Willie, you know we must firmly believe
That the presents we ask for we're sure to receive;
You must wait just as still till I say the 'amen,'
And by that you will know that your turn
    has come then.

"Dear Jesus, look down on my brother and me
And grant us the favor we are asking of Thee:
I want a wax dolly, a tea set and ring,
And an ebony workbox that locks with a spring.
Bless Papa, dear Jesus, and cause him to see
That Santa Claus loves us far better than he.
Don't let him get fretful and angry again
At dear brother Willie and Annie. Amen."

"Please, Desus, let Santa Taus tum down tonight
And bring us some presents before it is light.
I want he should div me a nice little sled
With b'ite shiny runners and all painted red;
A box full of tandy, a book and a toy,
Then Desus, I'll be a dood boy. Amen."

Their prayers being ended, they raised up
    their heads,
    And with hearts light and cheerful again
sought their bed.
They were soon lost in slumber, both peaceful
    and deep
And with fairies in dreamland were roaming
    in sleep.

Eight, nine, and the little French clock had
    struck ten,
Ere the father had thought of his children again:
He seems now to hear Annie's suppressed sighs,
And to see the big tears stand in Willie's blue eyes.
"I was harsh with my darlings," he mentally said,
"And should not have sent them so early to bed;
But then, I was troubled, my feelings found vent,
For bank stock today has gone down ten percent.

But of course they've forgotten their troubles ere this.
And that I denied them the thrice-asked-for-kiss.
But just to be sure I'll steal up to their door,
For I never spoke harsh to my darlings before."
So saying, he softly ascended the stairs
And arrived at the door to hear both of
    their prayers.

His Annie's "Bless Papa" draws forth the big tears,
And Willie's grave promise falls sweet on his ears.
"Strange, strange, I'd forgotten," he said with a sigh,
"How I longed when a child to have Christmas
    draw nigh.
I'll atone for my harshness," he inwardly said,
"By answering their prayers ere I sleep in my bed."

Then he turned to the stairs, and softly
    went down,
    Threw off velvet slippers and silk
    dressing gown,
Donned hat, coat, and boots, and was out in
    the street.
A millionaire facing the cold, driving sleet.
Nor stopped he until he had bought everything,
From a box full of candy to a tiny, gold ring.
Indeed, he kept adding so much to his store
That the various presents outnumbered a score.
Then homeward he turned with his holiday load,
And with Aunt Mary's aid in the nursery
    was stowed.

Miss dolly was seated beneath a pine tree,
By the side of a table spread out for a tea.
A workbox well-filled in the center was laid,
And on it the ring for which Annie had prayed.
A soldier in uniform stood by a sled,
With bright, shining runners, and all painted red.
There were balls, dogs, and horses, books
    pleasing to see
And birds of all colors were perched in the tree;
While Santa Claus, laughing, stood up on the top.

And as the fond father the picture surveyed,
He thought for his trouble he had amply been paid;
And he said to himself, as he brushed off a tear,
I'm happier tonight than I've been for a year.
I've enjoyed more true pleasure than ever before,

What care I if bank stock falls ten percent more?
Hereafter I'll make it a rule, I believe,
To have Santa Claus visit us each Christmas Eve.
So thinking, he gently extinguished the light,
Then tripped down the stairs to retire for the night.

As soon as the beams of the bright morning sun
Put the darkness to flight, and the stars, one
    by one,
Four little blue eyes out of sleep opened wide,
And at the same moment the presents espied.
Then out of their bed they sprang with a bound.
And the very gifts prayed for were all of
    them found.
They laughed and they cried in their innocent glee
And shouted for Papa to come quick and see
What presents old Santa Claus brought in
    the night,
(Just the things that they wanted) and left
    before light.

And now," added Annie, in a voice soft
    and low,
"You'll believe there's a Santa Claus, Papa,
    I know."
While dear little Willie climbed up on his knee,
Determined no secret between them should be.
And told in soft whispers how Annie had said
That their dear, blessed mamma so long ago dead
Used to kneel down and pray by the side of
    her chair,
And that God up in heaven had answered
    her prayer!
"Then we dot up and prayed dust as well as
    we tould,
And Dod answered our prayers; now wasn't
    He dood?"

"I should say that He was if He sent you all these,
And knew just what presents my children
    would please."
(Well, well, let him think so, the dear little elf;
Would be cruel to tell him I did it myself.)
Blind father! Who caused your proud heart to relent:
And the hasty words spoken so soon to repent?
'Twas Lord Jesus who bade you steal softly upstairs.
And made you His agent to answer their prayers.

Two generous young hearts arrive with their offerings. Photo by Dianne Dietrich Leis.

Our Christmas Odyssey

Thomas M. Boyd

On Christmas Eve, my mother and her friends stuffed fresh fruit and assorted groceries into worn bushel baskets, then crammed them into what would soon become a convoy of cars heading into the far reaches of Gloucester County, a part of Virginia's Tidewater, which was shoelaced by four rivers, with two hundred and twenty-seven square miles of flat, sandy earth–and, in the 1950s, one stoplight. Even though Colonial Williamsburg and the traditional sights and sounds of Christmas were in full array a mere thirty miles away, holidays in the country were always more muted and the underprivileged less visible.

My mother took special delight from including toys with each basket, each individually addressed. "This might be the only present those children will receive," she would say as she carefully wrapped each item in preparation for the journey, "and they will appreciate it more than you can ever know." Where I grew up, we were expected to share what we had, from the clothes my brother wore after me, to the availability of firewood, to the single telephone line we used with five other families, to the Christmas spirit.

Our odyssey often took us deep into the county, where poor families—both black and white—lived in dilapidated shacks veiled by walls of pine trees or in houses perched on cement blocks to protect them against sudden high tides, and where families either toiled in someone else's fields or fished the salt marshes near Guinea Island for crabs and oysters to sell to the restaurants and the tourists in Williamsburg or Yorktown.

I especially remember my first such tour the Christmas Eve when I was ten; the winter sky was uncharacteristically dark. The icy air, made worse by a steady, inhospitable wind, caused me to tighten the collar of my coat and, when I got into our car, crouch in front of the heater until its warm exhaust eventually spread beyond the dashboard to the cold vinyl bench seat beneath me.

We lived in a part of the country where brightly decorated trees could be seen through picture windows inside simple, rectangular one- or two-story houses ringed by colored lights. Plastic reindeer sometimes pranced outside, beside nativity scenes lit by spotlights. But on this evening, we were headed somewhere very different. Once we left the main road, we followed dark, winding, single-lane roads surrounded by a landscape occasionally punctuated by the outlines of darkened houses. The ebony sky blended with the pines to create the effect of driving through a long tunnel penetrated only by the reach of our headlights. Eventually, we came to a dirt road that began on the other side of a broken culvert. As the car slowly turned, our wheels traced ruts so deep that our hubcaps rubbed against the frozen crust and

emitted an eerie, grinding noise. The narrow lane was just wide enough for us to pass and, as our car moved forward, the undergrowth began to scrape against its sides.

A few yards in, our headlights fixed on the figure of a lone man clothed only in blue overalls and a gray sweatshirt in the twenty-degree air. He was slapping himself with his bare hands to keep warm. He had been waiting for us.

My mother got out immediately and spoke to him while I sat inside. After I got out, she brought me over to the man and introduced us. I still remember how completely his mammoth hand swallowed mine, how rough and hard and cold it was, and how, as he spoke, his breath left his mouth like steam escaping from a railroad engine. With my mother's eyes prompting me, I offered to help him remove the baskets from the car. Throughout he said very little, but when he did, his voice, bathed in the familiar rhythms of the country, was soft and gentle.

After he placed the baskets on the road in front of our headlights, the gaily wrapped presents to his children were visible atop the canned goods and powdered milk. I offered to help him carry the baskets into his house. He looked at me for an instant, and then at my mother, before politely declining. "I can manage alone, thanks all the same," he said, and I thought I saw a smile slide across his mouth. He lifted both baskets with a grunt, and as his form eventually merged with the night, I wondered what kind of a Christmas he and his family would have. Once back in the car, with feeling returning to my hands and feet, I kept thinking about him and how cold it was. "Why," I asked my mother, "did he meet us in the middle of the woods? Why didn't we just drive up the lane to his house?"

"Because," my mother answered, her face half visible in the glow of the dashboard, "he wanted us to meet him here." She said no more, but as she backed the car toward the paved road, I sensed in her shadowed face the serenity that always made the Christmas season so precious to her. She instinctively knew what it would take years for me to learn or understand—that Christmas is more than a religious holiday; it is a state of being, and its joys are best seen in the wonder and excitement found in the eyes of a child.

Devotions FROM THE Heart

Pamela Kennedy

Therefore as ye abound in every thing, in faith, and utterance, and knowledge, and in all diligence, and in your love to us, see that ye abound in this grace also. 2 Corinthians 8:7

THE GRACE OF GIVING

What could be more central to our celebration of Christmas than giving? Deciding upon just the right gift, making it or buying it, wrapping and presenting it occupies much of our pre-holiday time. For some, giving is an act of joy, for others a duty, and for a few, a way to level accounts and repay obligations. But if we look carefully at the many participants in that first Christmas two thousand years ago, we see giving of a different sort. It is an act of grace involving the heart and will, not the pocketbook.

At the beginning of the Christmas story, Mary willingly decided to give not only her heart, but her body as a gift to God. Without this act of giving, she never would have experienced the joy of nurturing the Son of God. Then Joseph had to be willing to give up his pride and accept the angel's words that his betrothed was with child because of an act of the Holy Spirit—not the will of a man. As a couple, these two newlyweds were willing to give up the comfort and security of Nazareth and travel to Bethlehem in accordance with both civil law and the words of Micah when he prophesied that the Messiah would come from this ancient town. Once they arrived at their destination, they had to give up any expectations they had for comfortable accommodations and lodge instead in a stable among livestock.

In order to come to earth as our Saviour, Jesus willingly gave up His heavenly honors and submitted Himself to the restrictions of humanity—hunger, thirst, pain, and disappointment. When the shepherds first heard the angel's announcement, they chose to give up their fear and travel to see the wonder revealed by the Lord. And having seen the holy Infant, they gave up their timidity and shared the wonderful news with everyone they encountered.

Far away, in the East, sages left the comfort of their towers and books, giving themselves to a quest for truth that would take them thousands of miles and several months of difficult travel. And when they finally found the object of their search, they gave gifts from their hearts, signifying the Lord's worth and destiny.

We miss the true importance of Christmas when we consider giving only in the context of wrapped presents under a tree. True Christmas giving is so much more. It involves experiencing the grace God expressed to us when He sent Christ. This is the grace of true giving: the willingness to give up our pride and our plans in order to participate in God's purposes. It might involve giving time to serve someone in need, forgiving a wrong in order to mend a relationship, or relinquishing a right so another is honored. In response to His generous love to you, what gift of grace are you willing to give to God this Christmas?

Dear Heavenly Father, I thank You for the gift of Your Son, Jesus Christ. This Christmas help me to experience the grace of giving from a willing heart to my family and my community and thus share in the blessings of that first Christmas in Bethlehem.

San Felipe De Neri Church glows for Christmas Eve in Albuquerque, New Mexico's Old Town. Photo by Jonathan A. Meyers/FPG.

THE SHEPHERD

John Davenport Womack

I do not think I'm likely to forget
The brilliance of the star that blazed that night,
And in my ear the song's resounding yet
Of that celestial choir whose voices bright

With hope and promise filled the shining air;
Rang from the nestling hills, rang from the earth
Where slept our flocks that night, all unaware
These voices heralded a Saviour's birth.

We went unto the stable where He lay
And my poor gift of love placed at His feet.
He smiled on me. The place grew bright as day,
And there was peace, ineffable and sweet.

SHEPHERD BOY, SHEPHERD BOY

John C. Bonser

Waken, waken, shepherd boy,
from your restless sleep
in that field near Bethlehem
where you tend your sheep.

Listen, listen, shepherd boy,
to an angel's voice:
"Unto earth a Child is come;
in His birth rejoice!"

Hasten, hasten, shepherd boy,
where His star shines bright;
do not fear to leave your flock,
lambs are safe tonight.

Worship, worship, shepherd boy,
from His realm above,
little Lamb of God who sleeps
in the arms of love.

A shepherd tends his winter flock in WHEN THE WEST WITH EVENING GLOWS *by British artist Joseph Farquharson (1846–1935). Image from City of Bristol Museum and Art Gallery, England/Bridgeman Art Library, London/Superstock.*

The Prophecies

For unto us a child is born, unto us a son is given: and the government shall be upon his shoulder: and his name shall be called Wonderful, Counsellor, The mighty God, The everlasting Father, The Prince of Peace. Of the increase of his government and peace there shall be no end, upon the throne of David, and upon his kingdom, to order it, and to establish it with judgment and with justice from henceforth even for ever. The zeal of the LORD of hosts will perform this.

ISAIAH 9:6, 7

But thou, Bethlehem Ephratah, though thou be little among the thousands of Judah, yet out of thee shall he come forth unto me that is to be ruler in Israel; whose goings forth have been from of old, from everlasting. MICAH 5:2

And there shall come forth a rod out of the stem of Jesse, and a Branch shall grow out of his roots: And the spirit of the LORD shall rest upon him, the spirit of wisdom and understanding, the spirit of counsel and might, the spirit of knowledge and of the fear of the LORD. ISAIAH 11:1, 2

LEFT: *Detail from* CHRIST IN GLORY *by artist Domenico Ghirlandaio (1448–1494). Image from Pinacoteca, Volterra, Italy/Superstock.*
ABOVE: *Detail of angels from Ghirlandaio's* ADORATION OF THE MAGI. *Image from Florence, Italy/Scala/Art Resource, New York.*

The Annunciation

And in the sixth month the angel Gabriel was sent from God unto a city of Galilee, named Nazareth, To a virgin espoused to a man whose name was Joseph, of the house of David; and the virgin's name was Mary. And the angel came in unto her, and said, Hail, thou that art highly favoured, the Lord is with thee: blessed art thou among women.

And when she saw him, she was troubled at his saying, and cast in her mind what manner of salutation this should be. And the angel said unto her, Fear not, Mary: for thou hast found favour with God. And, behold, thou shalt conceive in thy womb, and bring forth a son, and shalt call his name JESUS. He shall be great, and shall be called the Son of the Highest: and the Lord God shall give unto him the throne of his father David: And he shall reign over the house of Jacob for ever; and of his kingdom there shall be no end.

Then said Mary unto the angel, How shall this be, seeing I know not a man? And the angel answered and said unto her, The Holy Ghost shall come upon thee, and the power of the Highest shall overshadow thee: therefore also that holy thing which shall be born of thee shall be called the Son of God.

LUKE 1:26–35

ANNUNCIATION *by artist Domenico Ghirlandaio (1448–1494). S. Maria Novella, Florence, Italy. Image from Scala/Art Resource, New York.*

The Birth of Christ

And it came to pass in those days, that there went out a decree from Caesar Augustus, that all the world should be taxed. And all went to be taxed, every one into his own city.

And Joseph also went up from Galilee, out of the city of Nazareth, into Judaea, unto the city of David, which is called Bethlehem; (because he was of the house and lineage of David:) To be taxed with Mary his espoused wife, being great with child.

And so it was, that, while they were there, the days were accomplished that she should be delivered. And she brought forth her firstborn son, and wrapped him in swaddling clothes, and laid him in a manger; because there was no room for them in the inn.

LUKE 2:1, 3–7

Detail from ADORATION OF THE MAGI *by artist Domenico Ghirlandaio (1448–1494).*
Image from Uffizi, Florence, Italy/Scala/Art Resource, New York.

The Adoration
of the Shepherds

And there were in the same country shepherds abiding in the field, keeping watch over their flock by night. And, lo, the angel of the Lord came upon them, and the glory of the Lord shone round about them: and they were sore afraid. And the angel said unto them, Fear not: for, behold, I bring you good tidings of great joy, which shall be to all people. For unto you is born this day in the city of David a Saviour, which is Christ the Lord.

And this shall be a sign unto you; Ye shall find the babe wrapped in swaddling clothes, lying in a manger. And suddenly there was with the angel a multitude of the heavenly host praising God, and saying, Glory to God in the highest, and on earth peace, good will toward men. And it came to pass, as the angels were gone away from them into heaven, the shepherds said one to another, Let us now go even unto Bethlehem, and see this thing which is come to pass, which the Lord hath made known unto us.

And they came with haste, and found Mary, and Joseph, and the babe lying in a manger.

Luke 2:8–16

Detail from ADORATION OF THE SHEPHERDS *by artist Domenico Ghirlandaio (1448–1494).*
Image from Saint Trinity, Florence, Italy/Superstock.

The Adoration of the Magi

Now when Jesus was born in Bethlehem of Judaea in the days of Herod the king, behold, there came wise men from the east to Jerusalem, Saying, Where is he that is born King of the Jews? for we have seen his star in the east, and are come to worship him.

Then Herod, when he had privily called the wise men, enquired of them diligently what time the star appeared. And he sent them to Bethlehem, and said, Go and search diligently for the young child; and when ye have found him, bring me word again, that I may come and worship him also.

When they had heard the king, they departed; and, lo, the star, which they saw in the east, went before them, till it came and stood over where the young child was. When they saw the star, they rejoiced with exceeding great joy. And when they were come into the house, they saw the young child with Mary his mother, and fell down, and worshipped him: and when they had opened their treasures, they presented unto him gifts; gold, and frankincense, and myrrh.

Matthew 2:1, 2, 7–11

Detail from Adoration of the Magi *by artist Domenico Ghirlandaio (1448–1494).*
Image from Florence, Italy/Scala/Art Resource, New York.

The Oxen

Thomas Hardy

Christmas Eve, and twelve of the clock.
"Now they are all on their knees,"
An elder said, as we sat in a flock,
by the embers in fireside ease.

We pictured the meek mild creatures, where
They dwelt in their strawy pen,
Nor did it occur to one of us there
To doubt they were kneeling then.

So fair a fancy few would weave
In these years! Yet, I feel
If someone said, on Christmas Eve,
"Come; see the oxen kneel

"In the lonely barton by yonder coomb,
Our childhood used to know,"
I should go with him in the gloom,
Hoping it might be so.

A trio of barns provides shelter for animals on a secluded Idaho farm. Photo by Steve Bly/International Stock.

Pamela Kennedy

Art by Pat Thompson

THE PERFECT GIFT

Last September, I was contacted by a member of my mother-in-law's church and asked to be the speaker at their annual women's dinner in December. It was an honor I quickly accepted. I enjoy speaking and especially looked forward to an opportunity to give back something to a group of women who had often prayed for my family.

Looking for a fresh slant on the Christmas story, I poured over the Biblical accounts of the nativity. Re-reading Luke, I was struck with the realization that Mary's acceptance of God's gift brought her a lot of difficulties as well as joy. She had to deal with Joseph's doubts. Then I suspect that it wasn't easy explaining her unique situation to the neighbors in Nazareth. As her Son grew, there were other obstacles to overcome, misunderstandings to endure and, of course, the great grief of the crucifixion. Accepting God's gift didn't mean smooth sailing for Mary and, the more I studied, I realized that anytime anyone in Scripture received a gift from God, there were complications. What also became clear was that as people accepted the complex gifts God offered, God's grace began to flow into their lives with a new and wonderful abundance. We should then learn to embrace the difficulties of life more as gifts than problems. I was off and running with my Christmas talk.

Things were shaping up nicely when, just a few days before the Christmas banquet, I recognized a familiar scratchiness in my throat. That afternoon the delighted program chairwoman called to announce they were adding three more tables to accommodate even more ladies. She also reported that the table decorations were beautiful and a crew of fifteen was busy preparing all the condiments and desserts. I gulped and cheerfully assured her that everything was ready at my end. After hanging up, I dropped to my knees and told God if He could just forestall this cold for three days, I'd be happy to let Him give me pneumonia as a payback.

Apparently God didn't think much of my offer, and three days later I woke up unable to raise my voice above a whisper. When my mother-in-law called that morning and heard, or rather, didn't hear me, she told me she was activating the prayer chain and hung up quickly. All day long I reviewed my notes, sucked on throat lozenges, drank quarts of honey-lemon tea, and hoped the ladies at the church were locked in their prayer closets.

By six o'clock we were at the church. I smiled and nodded a lot and was ushered to the front row in the sanctuary where I lip-synced during the carols and prayed fervently for a miracle. Dinner was scheduled after the singing, and then everyone would return to the sanctuary to hear me speak—or so they thought.

As we settled at our beautifully decorated tables in the fellowship hall, we were served beverages and salads by the deacons, dressed for the occasion in tuxedo slacks, pleated shirts, vests, and bow ties. They had gone all out to make this a special evening, and I felt more desperate every minute. My table-mates chatted cheerfully and spoke encouragingly of the Lord's provision.

After our salad plates were removed, it became evident that there was a problem with the main course. The men kept refilling coffee cups and bread baskets, but the wild rice and Cornish hens remained sequestered somewhere in the kitchen. Evidently, the cook had not planned on the two hundred hens being partially frozen. After a half-hour, the worried program chairman asked me if I would mind speaking before dinner there in the fellowship hall since the main course was still not ready and needed another hour in the ovens. The poor woman could probably see her chairwomanship coming to a swift end. She had a speaker who could hardly whisper, a crowd of starving guests, a weeping cook, and hundreds of raw Cornish game hens.

I dashed out to retrieve my notes from the podium in the sanctuary. En route I grabbed a nattily dressed deacon and managed to communicate that I needed something to put my notes on, a big glass of water, and a very good microphone delivered to the stage in the fellowship hall within three minutes.

By the time I returned, all was ready. After a brief introduction, the program chairman handed me the microphone. I took a deep breath and began. When I croaked my first few words the room became unbelievably still as the women realized I was struggling with laryngitis. In very low, vacillating tones I related how God's gifts often include difficulties. I reminded them of Mary and the unexpected complications of mothering God's Son. I spoke of the disciples and how the gift of their time with Jesus also brought added challenges to their lives.

As I looked at the women seated at the tables, the deacons standing in the back waiting to serve, the cook dabbing at her eyes with a tissue, God gave me an unexpected revelation. This illness, the under-done dinner, the change in location for the program were all illustrations of the point I was trying to make. How would we respond? Would we see these things as a gift from God; an opportunity to experience His blessings in an unexpected way like Mary and the disciples? Or would we resort to disappointed complaining? Because of my weak voice, they had to listen even more carefully. Because of the delay in dinner, they weren't falling asleep with full tummies. Because we were in the hall and not the sanctuary, I was closer to them. And because of the speech topic that God had given me weeks earlier, we could all look at the things that had "gone wrong" not as disasters, but as special Christmas gifts from the Lord. As I spontaneously shared these thoughts I saw heads nodding in agreement.

I went to dinner to teach a lesson about how the things we see as problems in our lives could also be appreciated as gifts. When I finished I had experienced the lesson myself. My voice was completely gone after the last sentence of my talk, but as I sat down and looked at the perfectly browned bird on my plate, my heart sang a hymn of praise to God. Surely His gifts are always good.

Pamela Kennedy is a freelance writer of short stories, articles, essays, and children's books. Wife of a retired naval officer and mother of three children, she has made her home on both U.S. coasts and currently resides in Honolulu, Hawaii.

The Voice of the Christ Child

Phillips Brooks

The earth has grown cold with its burden of care,
But at Christmas it always is young.
The heart of the jewel burns lustrous and fair,
And its soul full of music breaks forth on the air,
When the song of the angels is sung.

It is coming, old earth, it is coming tonight;
On the snowflakes which cover thy sod,
The feet of the Christ Child fall gently and white,
The voice of the Christ Child tells out with delight
That mankind are the children of God.

On the sad and the lonely, the wretched and poor,
That voice of the Christ-child shall fall;
And to every blind wanderer opens the door
Of a hope which he dared not to dream of before,
With a sunshine of welcome for all.

The feet of the humblest may walk in the field
Where the feet of the holiest have trod;
This, this is the marvel to mortals revealed,
When the silvery trumpets of Christmas have pealed,
That mankind are the children of God.

A Christmas Carol

G. K. Chesterton

The Christ Child lay on Mary's lap,
His hair was like a light.
(O weary, weary was the world,
But here is all aright.)

The Christ Child lay on Mary's breast,
His hair was like a star.
(O stern and cunning are the kings,
But here the true hearts are.)

The Christ Child lay on Mary's heart,
His hair was like a fire.
(O weary, weary is the world,
But here the world's desire.)

The Christ Child stood at Mary's knee,
His hair was like a crown,
And all the flowers looked up at Him,
And all the stars looked down.

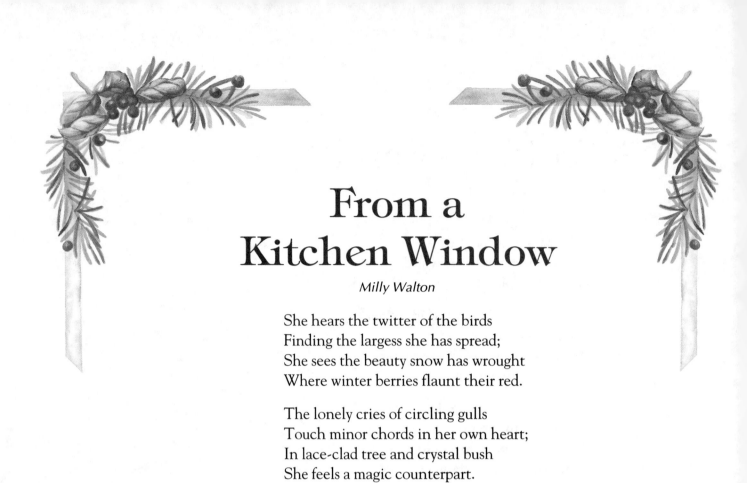

From a Kitchen Window

Milly Walton

She hears the twitter of the birds
Finding the largess she has spread;
She sees the beauty snow has wrought
Where winter berries flaunt their red.

The lonely cries of circling gulls
Touch minor chords in her own heart;
In lace-clad tree and crystal bush
She feels a magic counterpart.

She likes the snowman's pixie charm
Created by her wee one's hands
And looks up from her homely tasks
To share the whimsey he commands.

She has a kinship with the earth,
Though busy in her own domain,
And comprehends its noble plan
From just a kitchen windowpane.

*A snowman and snowchild seem to stroll toward a
woodland path in this photo by Jeri Gleiter/FPG.*

Handmade Heirloom

◆ ◆ ◆

An etched glass bowl holds memories of holidays past. Etched design by Eve Degrie. Photo by Christine M. Landry.

ETCHED-GLASS BOWL

Natalie Spence

I am generally timid when it comes to new crafts. I like to stick with what I know. I can knit. I can sew simple patterns. I can paint pottery at the local do-it-yourself studio. I have even, on occasion, stripped and refinished a small piece of furniture. But I have had some disastrous experiences with crafts. I took a class in rug-braiding once and ended up with nothing to cover my floor but a pile of colorful scraps and a braided circle about the size of a coaster. Once I even got ambitious about quilting. I bought fabric and batting and thread and needles and a quilting hoop only to find myself overwhelmed by the size of the queen-sized bed cover I had envisioned. Instead of a quilt, I have a basket full of fabric squares in beautiful shades of green, the sight of which continually reminds me to be cau-tious about beginning new projects.

Nonetheless, when I learned this fall that one of my oldest and dearest friends was getting married in December, I knew it was time to throw caution to the wind and try something new. Because, you see, my friend Mary is one of those naturally creative souls who never gives a gift that isn't handmade and never makes anything with her own hands that isn't perfectly beautiful. Her wedding would be my inspiration to try a new craft. And the collections of handmade gifts she had given me on various occasions—the grapevine wreath, the Irish knit afghan, the hand-painted bowls, the hooked rug, each of which adds daily beauty to my home—would be my inspiration to finish what I started and finish it well.

This is not to say that Mary is competitive or

judgmental about crafting; she is anything but, and she would receive any gift made with my hands with joy and pleasure and a stream of heartfelt compliments. I was the one feeling the need to measure up. So I thought big. I wanted something unique, something challenging, something beautiful. I decided on glass etching. It sounds complex and difficult, and it is a world apart from any of my previous craft successes. I set my sights on an etched-glass bowl. It would be smaller in scope, certainly, than a queen-sized quilt or a braided rug, but still unique enough to get noticed.

Intent on success, I started at the beginning and researched the history and the process of hand-etching on glass. The craft was pioneered in the late seventeenth century by Bavarian craftsmen. They discovered that by using hydrofluoric acid they could etch a beautiful pattern on window panes. The results were lovely, but the process itself was dangerous. The acid used in the etching released toxic fumes, making the craft inaccessible to most craftspeople and very dangerous to those equipped to do it. The heyday of this type of etching was the Victorian era, when mass-produced etched-glass tableware was enormously popular. In the late nineteenth century, etching became slightly more accessible when a new technique called sandblasting was discovered. The process, which used air pressure to propel sand, was safer; but it still require specialized equipment and was inaccessible to home crafters. In the mid-1900s, glass etching finally came into crafters' homes when a process using acid cream was discovered. Surprisingly, this acid cream is responsible for the entire etching process.

Glass etching today is quite easily done at home, although creating a detailed design requires painstaking work and immense concentration. To begin my project, I purchased a simple glass bowl and decided to create an etched pattern on the edges. In a moment of inspiration that I felt would certainly make Mary proud, I planned to repeat the leaf pattern from her wedding invitations as my etched design.

Once I selected the glass object to etch and decided on the design (pattern books are available to help with ideas), I covered the glass with clear contact paper. This paper is what etchers refer to as the resist, for it protects the covered portion of the glass from the etching process. After the glass was covered, I traced the design onto the contact paper with a sharp craft knife and peeled away the areas to be etched. Once the resist was prepared, I rubbed the acid cream onto the glass and left it to sit for ten or fifteen minutes. After a thorough cleaning, I removed the contact paper, and a beautiful etched design was left around the rim of the bowl.

There is more detail to the work than what I have described, and all directions must be followed carefully, for the acid cream still retains some of the toxicity of the old hydrofluoric acid. Books about the craft will give the basic details, and the instructions that come with the cream itself list the necessary precautions, including adequate ventilation and rubber gloves.

All in all, glass etching is a wonderful and accessible craft. It requires much concentration and precision, but it can also be completed in a single afternoon. I think that is why I found success with etching. New crafts are best taken on in small doses. Now that I have had this early success, I am thinking about etching a design on the corner of a glass tabletop. Working on a flat surface should make the project even easier than working on the curved side of the bowl.

What is my hope for this glass bowl? Of course, I hope to wow Mary, to get her to notice that I have not only tried something new, but have done it well. For, I must admit, I am impressed by the beauty of the bowl and the results of my first efforts at glass etching. Yet while measuring up to my dear old friend was my outward motivation, I realize, as I prepare to present the gift, that my real inspiration was the value of our friendship, and the joy I feel on the occasion of her marriage. I hope that my etched-glass bowl will find a place in her new home, as so many of her handmade gifts have found a permanent place in mine. Perhaps she will take it down from the shelf from time to time and think of me and all we have shared through the years. Maybe the leaf design from her wedding invitation will evoke warm memories of a happy day. And, I will admit, I hope she will find herself thinking that her dear old friend is much more creative and talented than she ever imagined.

While My Heart Listens

Mary C. Adams

My eyes delight in every dear familiar touch
Of Christmas in the house—
    the pine, the silver bells,
And all the rest. But let them not rejoice
    in these too much
Lest they miss seeing angels as their chorus swells
In adoration of the Child whose house was bare
Except that love beyond all other loves was there.

Let me not fret at baubles lacking for the tree,
At cookies to be baked and bundles left untied;
Nor mind the cluttered rooms,
    but sweep my spirit free
Of any pettiness, so He may come inside.
Let me forget all small and unimportant things
While my heart listens for the sound
    of angel wings.

Artist Marion Quimby offers a view of a traditional village at Christmas.

Poinsettia Versus Mistletoe

Blanche DeGood Lofton

Said the scarlet-mouthed poinsettia
To the grey-eyed mistletoe,
"No young folk ever look at you,
You're dull and drab, you know."

The mistletoe replied, "My dear,
Please remember this,
Though they can't help admiring you,
They let me watch them kiss."

A privilege 'tis then, you know,
To exercise time-honored rite;
When Christmas fires gleam and glow
When loving lips may pout, although
With other lips they oft unite—
'Tis merry 'neath the mistletoe!

—J. Ashby Sterry

Starlike poinsettia flowers cluster together in this photo by Steve Terrill.

Family Recipes

In seventeenth-century England, the presentation of the pudding at the end of the Christmas feast was the highlight of the holiday. This year, rekindle a centuries-old tradition in your home by trying these versions of Christmas puddings and custard. Then send us your own favorite holiday recipe. Mail a typed copy of the recipe along with your name, address, and phone number to Ideals Magazine, ATTN: Recipes, P.O. Box 305300, Nashville, Tennessee 37230. We will pay $10 for each recipe used.

Granny's Boiled Christmas Custard

Jeannine Long of Lebanon, Tennessee

3 whole eggs, well beaten
½ cup granulated sugar

¼ teaspoon salt
1 quart milk

1 teaspoon vanilla extract

In a medium bowl, combine eggs, sugar, and salt. Set aside. In a double boiler over boiling water, scald the milk. Add a small amount of milk to egg mixture and stir. Gradually add egg mixture to milk, stirring constantly. Cook until the mixture is thick enough to coat the back of a wooden spoon, about 20 minutes. Add vanilla extract. Cool and refrigerate until ready to serve. Makes 4 cups. Recipe may be doubled.

Rice Custard Pudding

Ethel Nilsen of Pomona, California

3 eggs, well beaten
2 cups milk
1 teaspoon vanilla

⅓ cup granulated sugar
¼ teaspoon salt
1 cup cooked rice

⅓ cup raisins, optional
Dash of nutmeg
Dash of cinnamon

Preheat oven to 350° F. In a large bowl, combine eggs, milk, and vanilla. Add sugar and salt; mix well. Stir in rice. Pour into a lightly greased, 10-by-10-inch baking dish. Sprinkle with nutmeg and cinnamon. Place the dish into a large shallow baking dish and place on oven rack. Pour hot tap water into larger dish to a depth of approximately ½ inch. Bake 1 hour, or until a knife inserted in the center comes out clean. Makes approximately 8 servings.

Baked Orange Date Pudding

Dorothy Rieke of Julian, Nebraska

- ¾ cup water
- 1 cup chopped dates
- 2 tablespoons butter
- 1¾ cups flour, divided
- 1 teaspoon baking soda
- ½ teaspoon cinnamon
- ¾ teaspoon salt
- ½ cup brown sugar
- 1 egg, beaten
- 1 teaspoon orange extract
- 1 10-ounce jar orange marmalade
- ½ cup chopped black walnuts
- Whipped topping

Preheat oven to 350° F. In a small saucepan, bring water to a boil. Stir in dates and butter. Remove from heat and set aside. Stir occasionally as butter melts.

Set aside 2 tablespoons of flour. In a medium bowl, sift together remaining flour, baking soda, cinnamon, and salt. Set aside. In a large bowl, combine brown sugar, egg, orange extract, and marmalade. Stir in date mixture. Slowly add dry ingredients, stirring until well blended. In a small bowl, combine walnuts with reserved flour. Stir walnuts into batter. Pour into an 11-by-7-inch baking dish. Bake 40 minutes or until toothpick inserted into center comes out clean. Serve with whipped topping. Makes 10 servings.

Holiday Plum Pudding with Lemon Sauce

Jean Gossett of Fayette, Alabama

- ½ cup plus 2 tablespoons butter, divided
- 1½ cups granulated sugar, divided
- 6 eggs
- ⅓ cup raisins
- ⅓ cup currants
- ⅓ cup chopped pecans
- 2 tablespoons flour
- 2 cups bread crumbs
- 2 teaspoons ground cinnamon
- ½ teaspoon ground cloves
- ½ teaspoon ground allspice
- ½ teaspoon grated lemon rind
- 1½ tablespoons lemon juice
- ⅛ teaspoon salt

Preheat oven to 375° F. In a large bowl, cream ½ cup butter with 1 cup sugar. Beat in eggs, one at a time. Set aside. In a small bowl, combine bread crumbs and spices. Slowly stir into butter mixture. Set aside. In a small bowl, combine raisins, currants, pecans, and flour. Stir into batter. Spoon batter into a greased, 11-by-7-inch baking dish. Bake 30 minutes or until toothpick inserted in the center comes out clean. Makes 10 servings.

To prepare sauce, in a double boiler over boiling water, combine remaining ½ cup sugar with cornstarch and water. Heat until mixture thickens. Remove from heat. Stir in 2 tablespoons butter, lemon rind, lemon juice, and salt. Serve over or with plum pudding. Makes about 1 cup.

An Old Friend

Johanna Ter Wee

When thoughts drift back to things we loved from long ago
The old wood range comes first to mind, its ruddy glow
And warmth leap through the years. Again we see
This old friend from the past—its personality.
The crackling and the snapping and the shimmery white heat,
The open oven door, a haven for our snow-chilled feet.
And what a wealth of savory odors greeted us each day
While the kettle sang a happy song to cheer us on our way.
When Mother polished it all shiny bright she'd say,
"It's smiling now." And at the close of each wintry day
We'd cast a backward glance, loathe now to leave its glow,
Anticipating chilly beds to which we need to go.
And though we now have modern stoves switched on and off at will,
Fond memories of the old wood stove have power to warm me still.

Praise God for Warmth

Edna Jaques

Praise God for warmth—for little rooms that hold
A warm bright fire, shelter from the cold,
For love that bids us welcome, hold us dear,
For peace that hovers like a pigeon near.

Praise God for warmth—O heart, for warmth and light
For walls that shut us from the lonely night,
For He who wandered homeless knows the way
Footsteps turn homeward at the close of day.

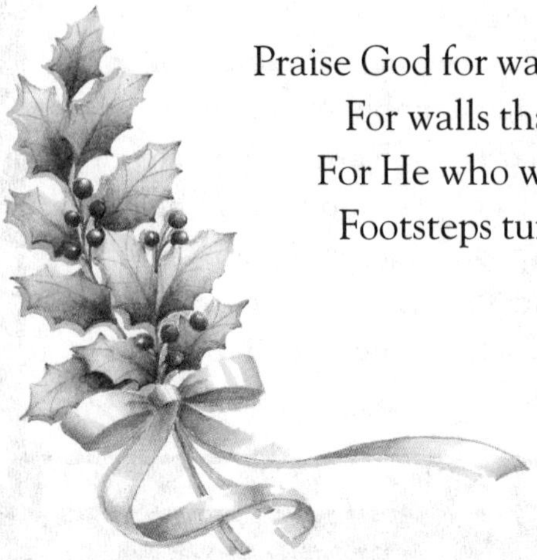

An old wood stove warmed many a family member in the Henry Fonda Boyhood Home in Nebraska. Photo by Jessie Walker.

OUR HERITAGE

IT CAME UPON THE MIDNIGHT CLEAR

Edmund Hamilton Sears

It came upon the midnight clear,
That glorious song of old,
From angels bending near the earth,
To touch their harps of gold.
"Peace on the earth, goodwill to men,
From heav'n's all gracious King."
The world in solemn stillness lay,
To hear the angels sing.

Still through the cloven skies they come
With peaceful wings unfurled;
And still their heavenly music floats
O'er all the weary world.
Above its sad and lowly plains,
They bend on hovering wing;
And ever o'er its Babel sounds
The blessed angels sing.

Yet with the woes of sin and strife
The world has suffered long;
Beneath the angel-strain have rolled
Two thousand years of wrong.

And man, at war with man, hears not
The love song which they bring.
Oh, hush the noise, ye men of strife,
And hear the angels sing.

O ye, beneath life's crushing load,
Whose forms are bending low,
Who toil along the climbing way
With painful steps and slow,
Look now! for glad and golden hours
Come swiftly on the wing.
O rest beneath the weary road
And hear the angels sing.

For lo! the days are hast'ning on,
By prophets seen of old,
When with the ever-circling years
Shall come the time foretold.
When the new heav'n and earth shall own
The Prince of Peace their King,
And the whole world send back the song
Which now the angels sing.

ABOUT THE TEXT

Edmund Hamilton Sears wrote the words to the beloved Christmas hymn It Came upon the Midnight Clear *as he sat in his study in Wayland, Massachusetts, one snowy December day in 1849. As he looked across the winter landscape, Sears's mind was full of the troubles of the nation as well as the approaching holiday. The prospect of a civil war loomed darkly on the horizon, and the words that Sears wrote that day reminded Americans that they could hear the message of the Christmas angels—peace on earth, goodwill to men—even in the most troubled times.*

Heaven's melodies are played in MUSIC-MAKING ANGEL WITH VIOLIN *by Italian artist Melozzo Da Forli (1438–1494). Image from Vatican Museums and Galleries, Rome/Superstock.*

STAR IN MY HEART

Mary E. Linton

Christmas is where you are . . . the chimes, the snow,
All make a setting for the heart aglow.
But Christmas is more subtle than all these,
Something beyond the shimmering of trees,
Something that reaches deep within the heart
To find your song, though we are far apart.
And if you hear my voice across the years
Singing the song we both have learned through tears,
Know that it holds the faith deep planted there,
Nourished by your dreams and our one prayer.
There must be miles between us, but a ray
Shines through the darkness and we know the way.
For where you are the Christmas star is bright,
And it is Christmas in my heart tonight.

STAR-FILLED

Ruth Shonyo Trask

Star-filled eyes that still reflect the light
That flourished over Bethlehem that night.
Voices carol-blending by a fire,
Echoing the Christ Child's angel choir.
A single candle's light—so soft, so low,
Borrowed from a tiny halo's glow.
The joy of giving presents large or small,
Time-treasured customs started at the stall.
Add hope, add love, the family 'round the tree,
And then you'll know what Christmas means to me.

A wreath and candle welcome family members home for Christmas. Photo by W. Talarowski/H. Armstrong Roberts.

Sleigh Ride

Martha D. Tourison

Beside the heart the sleigh bells hang
And wait my touch to sound again
That joyous ring that once we heard
As prancing steed tossed high his mane.

Our songs were gay, our laughter rang
Across the fields of glist'ning snow,
For we were young with carefree hearts
Those Christmas Eves of long ago.

"We're going home. We're going home."
Those singing bells would seem to say
As round the bend to lanterned door
Our cutter sparked its icy way.

And now the holly spray I twine
Between each shining silver bell.
I'm glad I lived in sleighing years
That only in my memory dwell.

A town prepares for the holidays in RAILROAD STATION
IN WINTER *by Konstantin Rodko. Image from Superstock Inc. Collection, Jacksonville/Superstock.*

in a one-horse open sleigh

FLORA

laughing all the way. . . . .

ANTIQUE VIOLINS

Neal Stewart

Many Christmases ago, my grandfather gave me a violin—he called it a fiddle—as a gift. I was disappointed. I wanted a bicycle and could muster little enthusiasm for a musical instrument. But it was a fiddle I got, along with his promise to teach me to play.

Fiddles and fiddling were very much a part of life where we lived, on Cape Breton Island, part of the Canadian province of Nova Scotia. It was an outgrowth of the predominantly Scottish heritage of the place. Since violins and their music were hard to escape in my childhood, escaping them was exactly what I had in mind. More to the point, I wanted to escape Cape Breton altogether. I tolerated my grandfather's lessons politely, but unenthusiastically, until the day I finally moved away from home.

I settled and raised my family in America, in the state of Vermont. Although my grandfather's fiddle remained untouched for decades, it remained with me through countless changes of life's course. I guess I didn't want a complete escape from my childhood after all. Predictably enough, as a grandfather myself, I long for those days on Cape Breton. More than a half century after that Christmas morning when a fiddle was waiting under the tree, that very instrument has become the centerpiece of a growing collection of violins.

It was on a summer visit to Cape Breton ten years ago that my passion for fiddles was awakened—as if it had lain dormant until that moment. There was a fiddlers' festival in the old neighborhood, and my wife and I spent a wonderful evening listening. The old songs evoked vivid images of my parents and grandparents, and of a time long past. Back at home, I took my fiddle from its case and tried to remember my grandfather's lessons. I was rusty, but not without skill. Finally, my grandfather's gift had captured my heart. In my retirement I have found the hours to practice that I could not spare as a teenager. I have become the fiddler my grandfather hoped I would be.

Since then I have done some research into the collecting of violins. I've learned that most serious collectors would not give my old Cape Breton fiddle a second look, but I have also discovered that I have no desire to own a Stradivarius. I am not that type of collector. I am not a classically trained musician searching for the perfect instrument to magnify my talents nor am I an investor looking to make a profit. I am simply an old man grown fond of nostalgia; I love violins because they take me back to a sweet and simple time in my life.

I own seven antique violins. Most come from my visits to Cape Breton, but I have purchased others in antique shops here in New England. Through research I know a little about what makes a fine instrument, and I know who were the favored violin makers of the nineteenth century in Eastern Canada, when most of my collection was built. There is only one piece of serious collectors' advice I always follow—I play a violin before I buy it. For it is, after all, not how the instrument looks or who made it or what style it is, but what kind of music it makes that truly matters. I don't have the ear of a concert violinist, but I know what I like, and that is a violin whose music reminds me of my grandfather's playing, of my childhood, and of home.

To someone unfamiliar with violins, the instruments in my collection look pretty much the same; they have only minor stylistic differences and slight variations in the hue of the wood. But each one holds a special meaning. Some I remember for where I purchased them, others for a unique story told to me by the previous owner. I take each one of them out from time to time and practice playing. I play for myself, for my wife, for our children and grandchildren, but I keep my first and favorite violin on display under glass in my family room. I take it out once a year, at Christmastime, and play an old Cape Breton folk tune I cannot name but have hummed throughout my life, ever since I first heard it during my grandfather's lessons long ago.

THE PERFECT NOTE

If you would like to collect antique violins, the following information will be helpful:

HISTORY

• The first bowed instruments were made in China in the 900s.

• Violins first appeared in the 1500s in Europe.

• The town of Cremona, Italy, was the center of violin making from the late 1500s into the 1600s. In this small city, the Amati family and, later, one of their students named Stradivarius crafted the world's greatest violins.

• Between five hundred and six hundred original Stradivarius violins remain today, about a third of the master craftsman's lifetime production. Most are in the hands of classical musicians, museums, and wealthy collectors.

• An enormous number of the violins available today were mass-produced during the late nineteenth-century. Their presence added greatly to the number of violin players, but not to the number of quality instruments available to collectors. Such instruments are often referred to as semi-antiques.

A collectible violin is ideal for playing favorite Christmas carols. Photo by Nancy Matthews.

TIPS FOR COLLECTORS

• Violins are the premium musical instrument for collectors and are viewed by many as a sound financial investment.

• Violins that are given good care can easily last hundreds of years. Ideally, instruments should be kept inside a specially made case and protected from sudden temperature changes and high humidity. Old and damaged violins should be taken to a professional restorer.

• Older does not automatically mean better in violins. Collectors value certain makers and the quality of a violin's music above the age of a particular instrument.

• Serious collectors should have a good knowledge of music or trust the opinion of someone who does. A violin has no value on the collector's market if it does not produce clear, beautiful music.

• "Fakes" and "ghosts" exist in the violin marketplace. The former are shoddy instruments marked with the name of a great maker; the latter are the same poor quality instruments marked with an invented name.

• Great deals are limited in collectible violins. The best instruments are held by musicians, collectors, and museums. For expensive violins, it is prudent to use a broker or an auction house.

NOTABLE VIOLINS

• In the Great Depression, Stradivarius violins were still fetching prices in the tens of thousands.

• Prices for the best works of the great names from the 1600s—Amati, Stradivarius, Bertolotti, Gagliano—have brought prices in the upper ranges of six figures.

A group of carolers raise their voices in GLAD TIDINGS *by William M. Spittle (1858–1917). Image from Fine Art Photographic Library Ltd./Baumkotter Gallery.*

A Carol for Christmas

Anna D. Lutz

Sing, oh sing, ye Christmas angels,
"Christ the Lord is born today."
Born to bring us full salvation,
Born to take our sins away.
Shine, oh shine, in all thy glory,
Shine, O star, in Bethlehem's sky.
Christ the Lord is born of Mary,
Born that men no more shall die.

Sing, oh sing, ye little children;
Christ is come, a tiny Child.
And in Bethlehem's straw-filled manger,
Mary cradles Jesus mild.

Sing, oh sing, ye men and women,
With the shepherds bend your knee;
Bring your hearts and love and praises.
Christ the Lord of Life shall be.

Sing, oh sing, then, all ye people,
Welcome Christ within your heart.
May He keep you in His Mercy,
And His peace and joy impart.
May His blessings crown our labors,
Keep us in His courts always.
So we'll sing with men and angels,
"Christ the Lord is born today."

Minstrels

William Wordsworth

The minstrels played their Christmas tune
To-night beneath my cottage-eaves;
While, smitten by a lofty moon,
The encircling laurels, thick with leaves,
Gave back a rich and dazzling sheen,
That overpowered their natural green.

Through hill and valley every breeze
Had sunk to rest with folded wings:
Keen was the air, but could not freeze,

Nor check, the music of the strings;
So stout and hardy were the band
That scraped the chords with strenuous hand.

And who but listened?—till was paid
Respect to every inmate's claim,
The greeting given, the music played
In honour of each household name,
Duly pronounced with lusty call,
And "Merry Christmas" wished to all.

Nancy Skarmeas

McRAE

ARTHUR FIEDLER

On the day that Arthur Fiedler died, the Boston Pops orchestra opened their program at Boston's Symphony Hall with a unique and moving tribute. The evening's conductor, Harry Ellis Dickson, gave the orchestra its opening cue and then stepped from the podium, leaving the musicians to perform a conductorless version of "The Stars and Stripes Forever," one of Fiedler's trademark pieces. Arthur Fiedler had conducted the Pops for just shy of fifty years; on this night in the summer of 1979, the show went on without him. His presence could be felt in every corner of Symphony Hall, and his image easily conjured up by any one of the musicians or audience members present on that night. With his trademark white attire and his shock of white hair, with his gift for uniting the staid world of classical music with the down-to-earth realm of popular culture, Fiedler had become as much of a Boston institution as the concerts he conducted. He had given his last cue to the musicians of the Boston Pops, but the orchestra would forever bear his unique signature.

Fiedler was a Boston native; but at his father's insistence, he had received much of his musical training at the Royal Academy of Music in Berlin. Fiedler grew up under the thumb of his domineering and hard-driving father, who demanded that serious, classical music be the focus of his son's energies. In 1915, at the age of twenty-one, Fiedler began his career with his hometown Boston Symphony Orchestra. He played piano, violin, and later viola.

Fiedler may have chafed at his father's controlling ways, but the son had inherited the elder Fiedler's ambition. In 1929 Fiedler boldly proposed a series of outdoor summer concerts for the Boston Symphony. The Esplanade Concerts, which he himself would conduct, were to be free evenings of music presented in an outdoor venue along the city's Charles River. The symphony accepted Fiedler's proposal, and the concerts drew large and enthusiastic crowds. He had guessed correctly that the general public wanted orchestra music to be entertaining as well as edifying.

The success of the Esplanade series probably won Fiedler the chance the following year to try his hand at conducting the Pops. The Boston Pops, short for Populars, began in 1885 and featured symphony musicians performing popular music. The Pops presented an annual summer series of concerts in hopes of boosting orchestra revenue and introducing a wider audience of Bostonians to concert music. In 1930 the Pops was floundering, and the Boston Symphony Orchestra looked to young Mr. Fiedler to revive it.

Revive it he did. Fiedler brought his sense of

music as entertainment, along with his prodigious skills and perfectionism, to the Pops. Under his leadership, the series soon became a treasured Boston institution. Fiedler's program featured orchestra arrangements of popular music, often complemented by celebrity guests, holiday themes, costumes, and a liberal dose of humor. The summer Pops evolved into a year-round series, with special programs for the Christmas season and the Fourth of July. The Independence Day concert alone would eventually draw hundreds of thousands of listeners to a night of music and fireworks, and Pops recordings under Fiedler's direction sold more than fifty million records. With Fiedler at the podium, the Boston Pops did everything its founders had envisioned—it brought the symphony to the people and brought financial stability to the Boston Symphony Orchestra.

What made Arthur Fiedler so successful and beloved? His musical gifts were undeniable. He possessed a perfect sense of pitch and an unmatched musician's ear. He was also a perfectionist who demanded the same precision from the musicians under his leadership. Fiedler appeared enthusiastic and light-hearted at the podium on concert nights, but he was demanding and focused during rehearsals. Many classical musicians disliked playing in the Pops, and many openly complained about Fiedler. They felt he was too willing to bring the symphony down to a common level. Although the music the Pops played might not be the serious classical fare the players preferred, it was what the audiences wanted; and it was, under Fiedler's direction, good music beautifully performed. Arthur Fiedler's popular music programs brought people into the audiences to hear fine music played; he introduced children to the look and sound of an orchestra, and he brought immeasurable publicity to the Boston Symphony Orchestra.

Anyone who lived in the Boston area during Fiedler's years with the Pops was familiar with Fiedler's favorite hobby, which seemed far-removed from his image as a conductor. As a young boy, Fiedler had become extremely interested in fire fighting and fire fighters. He had sneaked off to the neighborhood firehouse whenever he could escape the watchful eye of his father, and there he reveled in the exciting and heroic world of the fire fighters. It is easy to see why this world was appealing to him. At home he was expected to practice and practice, to play serious classical music, and associate mostly with other serious musicians. At the firehouse, he was among men whose talents and skills were physical, men who likely could not play a note on a viola, but who could climb a ladder through thick black smoke and rescue a baby from a burning building. As an adult, Fiedler held on to his obsession with fire fighting. He was made an honorary member of fire departments throughout the country, and he arranged for the Boston Fire Department to notify him of all major fires. On many a night, Fiedler rose from bed to drive to a fire scene and watch the Boston fire fighters work. Fiedler even developed an affection for Dalmatians, the traditional firehouse dog. This was a side of Arthur Fiedler not easily satisfied in the dry and serious world of classical music, a side that also found expression through the Pops.

Arthur Fiedler died in 1979, in his fiftieth year as conductor of the Boston Pops. He had made the annual Fourth of July Pops concert one of the most cherished events in the city of Boston, he had sold out the Christmas Pops concerts for years on end, and he had made the Boston Symphony orchestra a part of the lives of families throughout the region who might otherwise have never sat in a Symphony Hall audience. His name, his face, and his music will not soon be forgotten by the people of Boston, or by any true lover of music.

Nancy Skarmeas is a book editor and mother of a toddler, Gordon, who is keeping her and her husband quite busy at their home in New Hampshire. Her Greek and Irish ancestry has fostered a lifelong interest in research and history.

SYMPHONY HALL
Boston, Massachusetts

Norman Smith

Sometimes the greatest discoveries await us in our own backyards, invisible by nature of their familiarity. Such was the case for me with Boston's world-renowned Symphony Hall. I was born and raised in Boston and have lived in or near the city all my life, but I'd never set foot inside Symphony Hall. Not until this year, when I ventured into Boston two days before Christmas for an evening concert by the Boston Pops Orchestra, did I discover that the city I thought I knew inside and out still had a few surprises for me.

The Boston Pops, an offshoot of the Boston Symphony Orchestra, has been around for more than one hundred years. The undying appeal of the group is the combination of world-class classical musicians with a program of American popular music. Under conductor Arthur Fiedler, who stood at the Pops podium from 1930 to 1979, the Pops became a Boston institution and also won the distinction of being the most-recorded orchestra in the world. The Pops concert format of an opening of light classical music, followed by a classical or popular soloist, and a final selection of Broadway or movie music, big band favorites, or patriotic tunes was exciting and original at its inception, and has proven to have a timeless, universal appeal.

The evening of the Christmas Pops, I drove into Boston early and walked through the city to enjoy the lights of the season. Cities are wonderful places at Christmastime, and Boston is no exception. The trees on the Common—Boston's large, green, central park—were sparkling with tiny white lights, and the streets were bustling with shoppers. I am embarrassed to admit how many times I had walked down Huntington Avenue in the past and never given much thought to Symphony Hall. On this night it was hard to imagine feeling indifference toward this massive structure with its towering columns, arched windows, and intricately carved moldings.

I found the concert hall, bedecked for the season, to be every bit as elegant inside as the facade promised. The floor is wooden, as are the chairs, which are covered with a touch of leather, but nothing plush. Beautiful red leather doors open into the concert hall, and stately marble staircases lead from one level to another. The stage itself sits at the back of gently angled walls which allow the music to travel outward from the orchestra to fill the hall. Behind the stage is a pipe organ that reaches four stories high.

Symphony Hall was recently added to the American register of National Historic Landmarks. Musicians rank it among the top three classical music venues in the world and generally agree that its acoustics are the best in the United States. The founder of the Boston Symphony Orchestra commissioned the building in the 1880s as a performance hall for his orchestra. He had strict acoustical standards for the building's design and even went so far as to consult a Harvard professor of physics during the planning stages. Everything inside Symphony Hall exists for the purpose of improving sound quality. There is no plush carpeting and no seat padding to absorb the sound and no excess of nooks or recesses to trap it. Without a doubt, the original design was nearly perfect. Symphony Hall today looks almost exactly as it did one hundred years ago.

The Christmas program was in the best of the Pops tradition—a mix of classical and popular music, with a wonderful program of Christmas carols

Keith Lockhart conducts a holiday Pops concert at Symphony Hall. Photo by Michael Lutch, courtesy Boston Symphony Orchestra.

to close out the performance. The Pops is neither formal nor somber, and I found myself humming along to the familiar songs of the season, caught up in the joy and celebration. Of course, the sound quality was exquisite; every note, every instrument sounded through the hall with beautiful clarity.

Christmas at the Pops was truly an eye-opening experience for this Boston native. After the concert, the air outside was clear and cold, but the atmosphere was warm and festive. I had Christmas carols in my mind and the Christmas spirit in my heart. It was a perfect evening; proof that one need not stray far from home to experience the pleasure of discovering something new.

God's Winter Psalm

Lucille Chisham Campbell

Silver, shining silver,
Glistening, falling white.
Falling oh, so softly,
Twinkling in the light.

Every tiny flake falls,
Quietly and so calm.
Falling in silent rhythm
To God's winter psalm.

The Sound of Winter

Elizabeth Ann M. Moore

The creak and snap of frozen bough,
The sleighbell's frosty peal,
The muted murmur of the brook
Beneath its icy seal,

All speak the season's silvered voice;
There is no springtime now.
Across the sibilance of snow
It's winter country now.

And just across the snow-carved hill,
The river's icy bars
Reflect in silent solitude
The message of the stars.

Snow dusts the Benham Falls on Oregon's Deschutes River. Photo by Bruce Jackson/Gnass Photo Images.

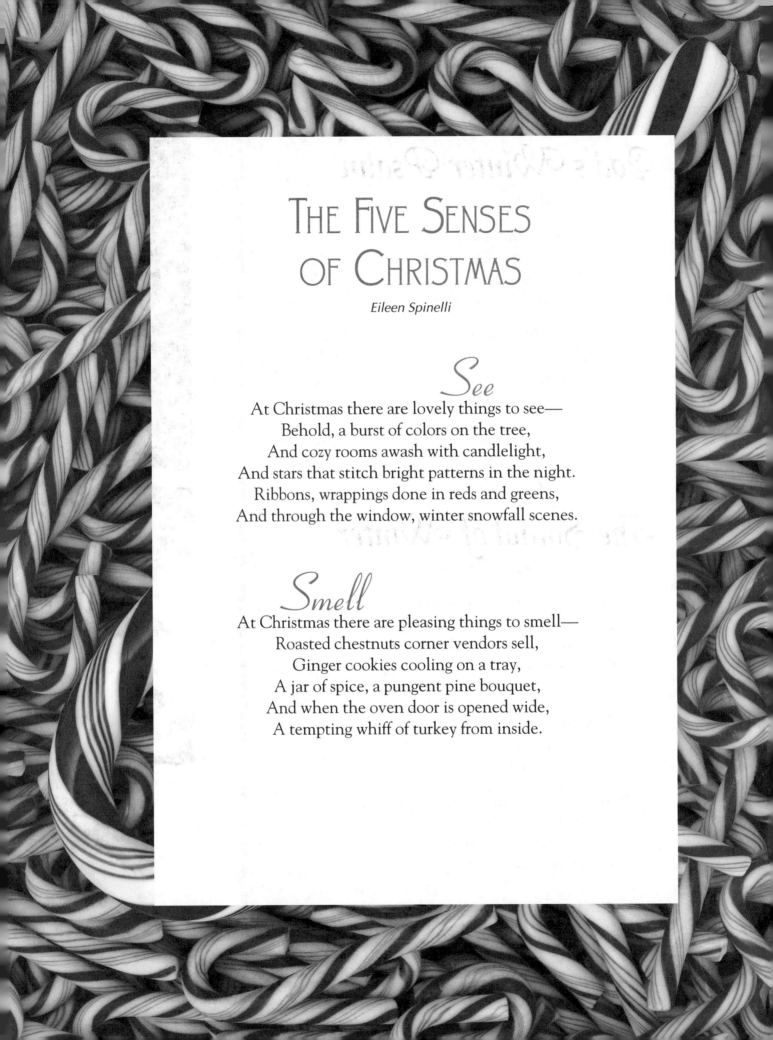

THE FIVE SENSES OF CHRISTMAS

Eileen Spinelli

See

At Christmas there are lovely things to see—
Behold, a burst of colors on the tree,
And cozy rooms awash with candlelight,
And stars that stitch bright patterns in the night.
Ribbons, wrappings done in reds and greens,
And through the window, winter snowfall scenes.

Smell

At Christmas there are pleasing things to smell—
Roasted chestnuts corner vendors sell,
Ginger cookies cooling on a tray,
A jar of spice, a pungent pine bouquet,
And when the oven door is opened wide,
A tempting whiff of turkey from inside.

Touch

At Christmas there are splendid things to touch—
Warm and fuzzy coats and hats and such,
Velvet vests and hand-knit slipper socks,
A gift that jiggles when you shake the box,
A friend, a snowflake delicate and frail,
A chunk of ice, a merry batch of mail.

Taste

At Christmas there are luscious things to taste—
A fruited stollen filled with almond paste,
A mug of cocoa or a glass of punch,
A minty candy cane for after lunch,
A juicy orange or a mellow pear,
Perhaps plum pudding, elegant and rare.

Hear

At Christmas there are joyful things to hear—
The sound of church bells ringing deep and clear,
The festive singing voices of a choir,
A snap of twigs, the crackling of a fire,
The story told at bedtime o'er and o'er
Of peace on earth, good will forevermore.

*Candy canes wait to trim a tree. Photo by Peter
Gridley/FPG International.*

BITS & PIECES

The winter winds whip icing white
And pile it on the lake.
They swirl each snow mound soft and light
Like frosting fluff on cake.
—Nadene M. Murphy

May our lives like the snowflake
Be a pure-white symphony
Until the chorus fills the earth
With peaceful melody.
—Sister M. Norbert

No snowflake ever falls
in the wrong place.
—Zeno, 335–263 B.C.

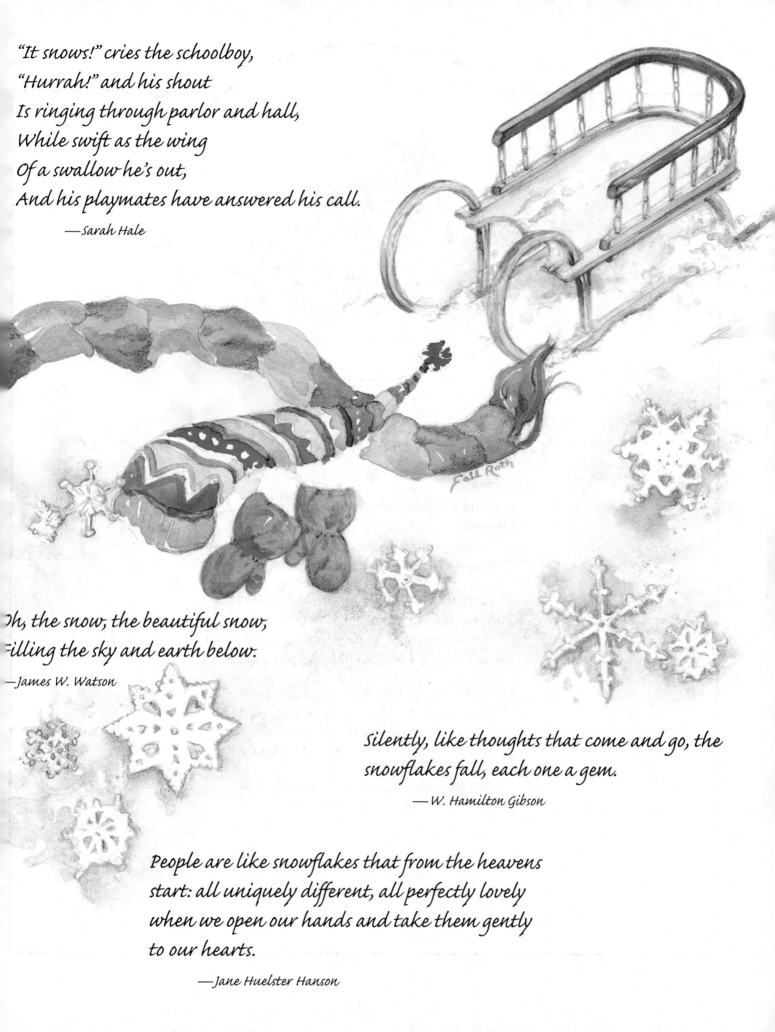

"It snows!" cries the schoolboy,
"Hurrah!" and his shout
Is ringing through parlor and hall,
While swift as the wing
Of a swallow he's out,
And his playmates have answered his call.
—Sarah Hale

Oh, the snow, the beautiful snow,
Filling the sky and earth below.
—James W. Watson

Silently, like thoughts that come and go, the
snowflakes fall, each one a gem.
— W. Hamilton Gibson

People are like snowflakes that from the heavens
start: all uniquely different, all perfectly lovely
when we open our hands and take them gently
to our hearts.
—Jane Huelster Hanson

Christmas Is More

Berniece Ayers Hall

Christmas is more than candle-lighted trees
Or stockings hung to bulge with mysteries,
More than a glowing fire on home's bright hearth
Or warm goodwill encircling the earth,

More than the joy of friendship and good cheer
Mirrored in eyes this magic time of year,
Or carols sung, or precious gifts we choose.
These things belong, but Christmas is good news

Of God's own love to us, a sacred place
With starlight shining on a Baby's face,
And seeking pilgrims of all centuries
In reverent silence gathered on their knees.

Christmas is all of these, and vastly more—
Hearts that are glad to worship and adore.

A fireside chair provides a cozy spot to rest after a day in the snow.
Photo by Michael Nelson/FPG International.

Readers' Forum

Snapshots from Our Ideals Readers

LEFT: Mary Meacham Fishburn of Nashville, Tennessee, shares this holiday photo of her great-niece, Mary Catherine Meacham, age eight months. Little Mary Catherine was happy to pose with her two adorable, and wiggly, Christmas puppies.

BELOW: Dressed in angel costumes, Rachel and Claire Grant, age two years and age eleven months, are revealing their true character to grandparents John and Ann Smithson of Starkville, Mississippi. Rachel and Claire live in Memphis, Tennessee.

ABOVE RIGHT: Andrew Van Dellen (age twenty-two months) takes his new sister Christina (age four months) on her very first toboggan ride at their home in Golden Valley, Minnesota. Luckily, the children's grandmother, Linda Van Dellen, lives nearby and never misses memories like this sledding adventure.

BELOW RIGHT: Aleisha Gardiner, who is three years old, had no complaints about the big snowstorm that arrived at her home in Troy, Maine, last year. The snapshot was sent to us by Aleisha's grandmother, June Gardiner of Unity, Maine.

Thank you Mary Meacham Fishburn, John and Ann Smithson, Linda Van Dellen, and June Gardiner for sharing your family photographs with *Ideals*. We hope to hear from other readers who would like to share snapshots with the *Ideals* family. Please include a self-addressed, stamped envelope if you would like the photos returned. Keep your original photographs for safekeeping and send duplicate photos along with your name, address, and telephone number to:

Readers' Forum
Ideals Publications Inc.
P.O. Box 305300
Nashville, Tennessee 37230

ideals

Publisher, Patricia A. Pingry
Editor, Michelle Prater Burke
Designer, Travis Rader
Copy Editor, Christine M. Landry
Editorial Assistant, Elizabeth Kea
Contributing Editors, Lansing Christman, Deana Deck, Pamela Kennedy, and Nancy Skarmeas

ACKNOWLEDGMENTS

HOLMES, MARJORIE. "The Perils and Pleasures of Winter" from "The Secret of the Christmas Tree" from *You and I and Yesterday* by Marjorie Holmes. Reprinted by permission of the author. JAQUES, EDNA. "Praise God for Warmth" from *Beside Still Waters* by Edna Jaques. Copyright © in Canada by Thomas Allen & Son Limited.

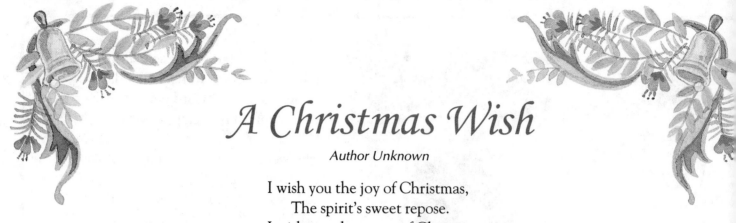

A Christmas Wish

Author Unknown

I wish you the joy of Christmas,
    The spirit's sweet repose.
I wish you the peace of Christmas
    To mark the old year's close.
I wish you the hope of Christmas
    To cheer you on your way,
And a heart of faith and gladness
    To greet each coming day.

The New Year

Grace Noll Crowell

The new year lies before us, white and clean:
    So many lovely days in which to live,
So many hours to spend like silver coins,
    So many precious moments God will give
For us to use in service and in love,
    In friendliness and sympathy, until
Our lives may be like fountains, lifting up
    To sparkle in the sunlight and to spill
In radiance and beauty all about,
    That other lives may catch the gleam and shine
Of spraying fountains, lifting, filled with light,
    That will be your life, friend, that will be mine.

O help us live so beautifully, God,
    This year of all the years, that we may be
Like showers of blessings, falling on mankind—
    Bright fountains, lifting high and clear to Thee.